Christian Jr./Sr High
2100 Greenfield [
El Cajon, CA 920

IN THIS SERIES

Auto Racing

Baseball

Basketball

Bodybuilding

Extreme Sports

Field Hockey

Figure Skating

Football

Golf

Gymnastics

Hockey

Lacrosse

Martial Arts

Soccer

Softball

Strongman Competition

Tennis

Track and Field

Volleyball

Wrestling

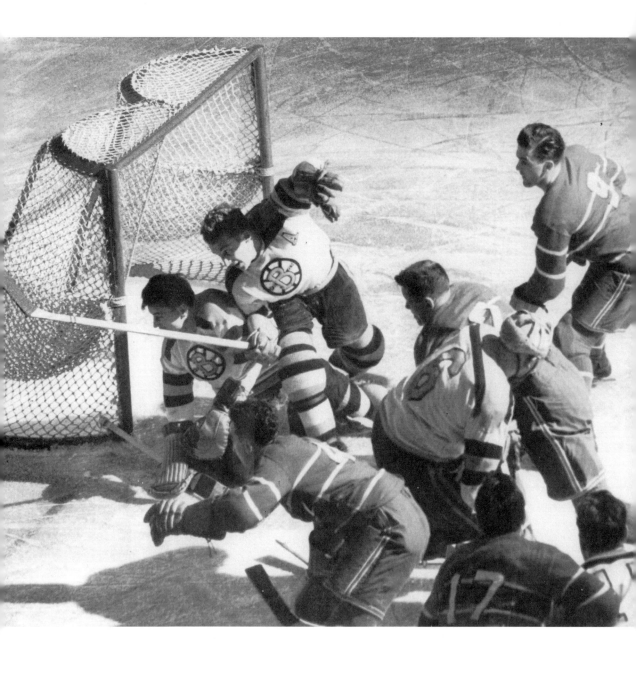

to **HOCKEY**

CARRIE L. MUSKAT

CHELSEA HOUSE PUBLISHERS
Philadelphia

Produced by Choptank Syndicate, Inc.

Editor and Picture Researcher: Norman L. Macht
Production Coordinator and Editorial Assistant: Mary E. Hull
Design and Production: Lisa Hochstein
Cover Illustrator: Cliff Spohn
Cover Design: Keith Trego
Art Direction: Sara Davis

3 5 7 9 8 6 4

Library of Congress Cataloging-in-Publication Data

Muskat, Carrie
        The composite guide to hockey / Carrie L. Muskat.
            p.   cm.— (The composite guide)
        Includes bibliographical references and index.
        Summary: Traces the story of hockey, from its beginnings, to its first stars,
    great teams, and championship games, to the notable players of today.
        ISBN 0-7910-4727-X (hardcover)
        1. Hockey — History — Juvenile literature.   [1. Hockey.]
    I. Title.   II. Series.
    GV847.25.M87 1997
    796.962 — dc21   97-28696
                                                                               CIP
                                                                               AC

CONTENTS

BIG GAMES

On March 23, 1994, at the Great Western Forum in Inglewood, California, Wayne Gretzky claimed his status as the greatest goal-scorer in the National Hockey League.

Before 16,005 cheering fans watching Gretzky's Los Angeles Kings and the Vancouver Canucks, Gretzky took a power-play cross-ice pass from Marty McSorley, his old Edmonton Oilers teammate. McSorley had pulled Vancouver goalie Kirk McLean out of the crease before passing to Gretzky, who skated in from the left circle to score on his first shot of the game at 14:47.

The goal was the 802nd of Gretzky's career, passing the record of 801 held by the Detroit Red Wings' legendary Gordie Howe. Howe had scored 801 goals in 1,767 games over 26 seasons. Gretzky set the record in his 1,117th game over 15 seasons.

Gretzky leaped for joy, raised his arms in triumph, and danced around the ice. His teammates rushed off the bench to surround him. The game was held up while Gretzky's wife Janet, his parents, Kings owner Bruce McNall and NHL commissioner Gary Bettman joined the jubilant record holder for a 10-minute celebration.

"You always were the Great One," Bettman said. "Tonight, you became the greatest."

The record was the 62nd of Gretzky's fabulous career. He owned every major offensive record in the hockey books. The career goal mark elevated him to a level achieved by a select few in their

Wayne Gretzky holds more offensive records than any other hockey player in history. In 1997 he teamed with former Edmonton Oilers teammate Mark Messier to lead the New York Rangers into the Stanley Cup playoffs.

sports: baseball's Hank Aaron (755 home runs), football's Walter Payton (16,726 yards), and basketball's Kareem Abdul-Jabbar (38,387 points).

Before the game Gordie Howe had called Gretzky to offer his encouragement. Howe had been Gretzky's idol since Gretzky first laced up skates as a youth in Brantford, Ontario. Gretzky tried to mimic Howe's style on the ice. He even attempted to copy the legend's thinning hair, telling his barber to cut a bald patch on his head. When Gretzky was 11, Howe presented an award to him at a banquet and advised the youngster to work on his backhand. Gretzky took the advice; the shot that broke Howe's record was a backhand shot.

"He was born to put the puck in the net," Howe said of Gretzky. After watching the record-breaking event on television from his home in Michigan, Howe suggested that Gretzky keep scoring until he reached 1,000 goals.

"I see 900, I see 1,000," Gretzky said. "I don't know if I'll get there, but I'll give it an effort. My life is hockey."

Hockey has provided its fans with many exciting historic moments over the years. As in most sports, the headlines usually go to offensive stars like the quarterback in football, the baseball sluggers, and the high-scoring basketball centers and forwards. Defensive stars get less attention. But few defensive players stand as alone or carry as big a burden as the hockey goalie.

Hockey is a specialized game. The wings and center are always on the attack. The defenseman's job is to stop the wings and center from getting near the net. The goalie's job is to stop the puck from going into the net. Once an attacker gets past the defense, only the goalie stands in the way of a goal. Sometimes it's a one-on-one contest; sometimes it can be a two- or three-on-one power play.

On the night of November 10, 1963, at the Detroit Olympic Stadium, a goalie shared the spotlight with a wing. For months, Detroit star Gordie Howe had been pressing to break the career scoring record of 544 goals set by Maurice Richard (Ri-SHARD). Howe had gone two weeks without a goal. At the same time, Detroit goalie Terry Sawchuk was closing in on the all-time shutout record of 94, held by George Hainsworth. On that night, with 15,027 fans urging him on, Howe, whose wrist shot was once timed at 114 miles an hour, snapped a second-period shot into the net from 25 feet to break the record.

The Red Wings won, 3–0, but Sawchuk's record-tying feat was overshadowed by Howe's. The Detroit goalie had to wait until January 18, 1964, to celebrate in his own spotlight. He made 36 saves in Detroit's 2–0 victory over the Canadiens at the Montreal Forum for his 95th shutout. Sawchuk, who used an unorthodox gorilla-like stance, finished his career with 103 shutouts. He felt his record was much more difficult to accomplish than the scoring record. Goals can be scored on fluke plays, yet the player received full credit. If a goalie makes a single mistake and lets a puck slip by, he has to wait until the next game to start his shutout bid all over again.

"You gotta play 60 minutes to get my record," Sawchuk said.

Bobby Orr, of the Boston Bruins, flies through the air after being tripped while scoring the winning goal against St. Louis goalie Glenn Hall in overtime to win the 1970 Stanley Cup.

Bobby Orr of the Boston Bruins revolutionized the defenseman's position. In the 1969–70 season, the 22-year-old Orr became the first defenseman to win the league scoring title. That year he became the first hockey player ever to win four individual trophies in the same season: the Norris Trophy for top defenseman; the Hart Trophy for most valuable player; the Art Ross Trophy as top scorer; and the Conn Smythe Trophy for MVP in the playoffs.

No defenseman had the grace and sheer drama that the Bruins' No. 4 displayed when he grabbed the puck and raced up the ice. In the 1970 Stanley Cup finals, Boston took a 3–0 lead over the St. Louis Blues, although Orr did not score a single goal in the three games. Game 4 at Boston Garden went into overtime.

Just seconds into the extra period, Orr took a pass from Derek Sanderson and flipped the puck past sprawling goalie Glenn Hall into the net. Bruins fans will never forget the joyous image of Orr, who was tripped on the play, flying through the air, his arms raised in celebration of Boston's first Stanley Cup championship since 1941.

"Bobby was a star from the moment they played the national anthem in his first NHL game," said Boston coach Harry Sinden.

Many stars have sparkled in professional hockey leagues since a group of Canadian skaters first put the field game on ice in the 19th century.

HISTORY OF THE GAME

Ice hockey is a Canadian game whose origins as a field game go back to the fifth century B.C. A marble relief in the Athenian acropolis in Greece shows two men "facing off." The men are holding sticks with a ball between them.

The game's name could stem from a playful Iroquois tribe. French explorers traveling up the St. Lawrence River saw the Indians hitting a hard ball with sticks and heard them saying, "Ho-gee." Another theory is that the game takes its name from the sticks or "hoquet," which in old French is the word for a shepherd's crook or staff.

Ireland, Scotland, England, Russia, and Scandinavia all have produced ball and stick games, and the Dutch invented the first metal ice skate in the early 17th century. Adventurous types combined the two. The city of Kingston, Ontario, claims it hosted the first ice hockey game in 1830, but the Canadian cities of Halifax, Nova Scotia, and Montreal also boast that they introduced the sport.

The term "ice hockey" was first recorded in 1875, describing a game played by two nine-man teams of McGill University students at the Victoria Skating Rink in Montreal.

The McGill students combined the rules of field hockey, lacrosse, and polo. The following winter, there was class competition at the university, and by 1881 the school had one formal hockey club and the Victoria Rink had another.

Long before indoor rinks were built, games similar to hockey were played on frozen rivers and lakes. Here a Dutch player of 1700 takes a timeout.

The Montreal Winter Carnival of 1883 held the world's first ice hockey tournament, showcasing the new game. Interest sparked the creation of the Amateur Hockey Association of Canada in 1886 with five member clubs: the Quebecs, the Ottawas, and three from Montreal.

The rules called for no body checks, a face-off when the puck went behind the goal, a two-hour playing time, nine players, and a referee. The game made a dramatic switch during the 1886 Montreal Winter Carnival when two players were unavailable and the teams used only seven men. Competitors discovered the play was much improved. They borrowed the position names from soccer: goalkeeper, point, cover point, rover, right wing, center, left wing. In 1911 the rover was eliminated, leaving six-man teams.

The fast pace of ice hockey was entertaining and its appeal resulted in barnstorming teams in the central Canadian provinces. In 1892, Canada's sixth Governor-General, Lord Stanley of Preston, announced that he would sponsor a trophy for the Canadian champions. The trophy,

Games played with sticks and a ball go back at least 2,500 years, as shown in this ancient Greek carving.

known today as the Stanley Cup, is the oldest award for professional athletes.

The first official Stanley Cup match was played March 22, 1894, in Montreal between the Montreal Hockey Club and the Ottawa Capitals. Montreal won 3–1 in front of 5,000 fans. The *Montreal Gazette* reported the ice was good for the championship game, but that "the referee forgot to see many things."

Some championship teams were unique. The Thistles of Kenora, population 10,000, represented the smallest town to win the Cup, doing so in 1907. The Montreal Wanderers were the first team to inscribe the names of all its players on the trophy. The Seattle Metropolitans were the first to carry the Cup across the border to the United States in 1917.

The trophy itself had trouble keeping up with the game. The bowl grew taller with the addition of more silver for more engravings. In 1947, it expanded in width to accommodate team names. One year, a drunken player booted the Cup into an Ottawa canal on a dare. A photographer's wife once used it as a flower pot. Pranksters have stolen it, and the celebrating Montreal Canadiens left the trophy in a snowbank after stopping to change a tire. The only time a Stanley Cup championship was not played was in 1919 because of a fatal influenza that infected several teams.

Professional hockey's official birthday is November 22, 1917. On that day, five men met in a hotel room in Montreal and organized a league of professional players to be called the National Hockey League.

Frank Calder, a 30-year-old transplanted British schoolteacher and sportswriter, was named the NHL's first president, a position he would hold for 26 years. In 1943, the NHL established the Calder Trophy, presented to the top rookie player.

The four original teams—Montreal Canadiens, Montreal Wanderers, Ottawa, and Toronto—began play on December 19, 1917. Joe Malone scored five goals to lead the Montreal Canadiens to a 7–4 victory over Ottawa, while the Montreal Wanderers beat Toronto 10–9, in front of a disappointing crowd of 700. Quebec took to the ice in 1919.

During the next 10 years, the NHL grew to 10 teams. In 1924, the first American franchise was awarded to Boston. The next year, the Hamilton Tigers went on strike, demanding $200 a man to play the winner of the Montreal Canadiens vs. Toronto series for the league championship. Calder said no and the players were suspended and fined $200 each—the exact sum they had tried to collect. The league then sold the team to New York City and the Canadiens were declared the Stanley Cup winners.

But the NHL teams were not the only ones competing for Lord Stanley's Cup. There also were teams in the Western Canada Hockey League, formed in 1921, and the Pacific Coast Hockey Association. In 1926, the Montreal Canadiens defeated the Victoria Cougars of the Western League for the Stanley Cup, marking the last time a team outside the NHL would challenge for the trophy.

As ice hockey evolved into a more organized game, its equipment improved. In the beginning, skaters used bone fragments as blades. In the 1880s, they tied metal skates to boots with thin leather harness straps. By the early

1900s, a skater could lace up a boot with the blade attached. Today they wear high-tech leather boots with plastic protection on the blade, extra toe padding, and a higher tongue.

Hockey sticks have developed over time as well from sturdy tree branches to feather-weight aluminum and wood models. Advanced designs created dangerous situations for goalies, who had to deal with faster skaters and even faster pucks aimed at them. Clint Benedict of the Montreal Maroons was the first NHL goalie to don a mask in a game back in 1930, wearing a crude leather covering to protect a broken nose. It would be nearly 30 years—and many more bruised cheeks and broken bones—before masks were used on a regular basis.

Except for the equipment and uniforms, ice hockey has changed very little since this game between New York and Jersey City teams in 1888.

Even though he never played a professional hockey game, Hobey Baker is often called "hockey's immortal American." Born in Wissahickon, Pennsylvania, on January 15, 1892, Baker played amateur hockey and was the captain of the Princeton University team in 1910. The team was jokingly known as "Hobey Baker and the Tigers." His stick handling was so accurate and natural that observers said once the puck was on his stick, he never needed to look at it again.

Baker also skated for the St. Nicholas Club in New York and helped his team upset the favored Montreal Stars in an exhibition game played in Quebec. Many of those watching the game—and especially the Stars players—could not believe Baker was not a Canadian. He was too talented, too skilled, they said. Baker helped to make the game popular in the United States.

Rather than play professional hockey, Baker chose to join the United States Air Force and became a distinguished combat pilot in World War I. But on December 21, 1918, one month after the war ended, he volunteered to test a plane that had had mechanical problems. The plane crashed, killing Baker at the age of 26.

The "grandfather of American hockey," he is remembered each year when the top collegiate hockey player in the country is presented a trophy in Baker's name.

Two-time winner of the Vezina trophy for the best goalkeeper, Charlie "Chuck" Gardiner was the goalie for the first two NHL All-Star teams in 1931 and 1932. He is shown with the gear and equipment used in 1921.

The National Hockey League's top goal-tender is presented a trophy named after Georges Vezina, who had acquired legendary status even before the league was created. Vezina did not learn how to skate until he was 18. He played goalie wearing his boots for an amateur club in his hometown of Chicoutimi, Quebec. Known as the "Chicoutimi Cucumber" for his cool demeanor, Vezina was discovered at the age of 23 by the Montreal Canadiens after he shut them out in an exhibition game.

Vezina played 16 professional seasons in the net, leading the Canadiens to their first Stanley Cup in 1916. His last NHL season, 1924–25, was one of his best. He posted a 1.87 goals against average, but Montreal fell short in the finals, losing to Victoria.

He had never missed a game in his entire career, but on November 28, 1925, Vezina pulled himself out of the net against Pittsburgh, saying he was bothered by chest pains and dizziness. Doctors diagnosed Vezina with tuberculosis and he never played again. One day in March 1926, he showed up in the Canadiens locker room, sat down beside his pads and skates, and cried. He asked for the sweater he had worn in his last Stanley Cup finals, then left. Vezina died March 24 that year. The next season, the NHL established a trophy in his honor. The first recipient was George Hainsworth, who replaced Vezina in the Canadiens' net.

Hockey's early years had their share of characters. Howie Morenz was dubbed "the Babe Ruth of hockey" by American sports-writers. He played the ukulele and considered himself quite the fashion plate, changing his clothes two or three times a day. He hated to lose, and after a disappointing game, Morenz would walk the streets at night. But it was his skating speed and intensity that brought fans out of their seats every time the "Stratford Streak" would begin an offensive surge.

The NHL founding fathers decided to use Morenz to help hype the game in hopes of expanding to the U.S. East Coast. There were professional hockey teams in Portland, Oregon; Spokane and Seattle, Washington; and Michigan and Pittsburgh. But the NHL was after the lucrative eastern market. Tex Rickard, a sports promoter who was building Madison Square Garden in New York, was invited to Montreal to see the flamboyant Morenz, hockey's first superstar.

Rickard was so impressed, he decided to install ice at the Garden and in 1926, New York had a pro hockey team. The Chicago Blackhawks and Detroit Cougars joined the Boston Bruins and Pittsburgh Pirates in the NHL's American Division that same year.

Morenz was more than a gimmick while skating for the Canadiens. In the 1924–25 season, he scored 27 goals in 30 games, and in 1929–30, he scored 40 goals in 44 games. The first player to win the Hart Trophy three times as Most Valuable Player in a season, he was eventually traded to Chicago, then New York, but returned to Montreal for the 1936–37 season. On Jan. 7, 1937, Morenz suffered a broken leg when he was knocked off balance and crashed into the boards. He died in his sleep March 8, 1937, officially from cardiac failure, but teammate Aurele Joliat says Morenz was devastated he would never be able to play the game again and "died of a broken heart."

Dubbed the "Babe Ruth of hockey," Howie Morenz was hockey's first superstar and played for Montreal, New York, and Chicago before his untimely death in 1937.

In the late 1920s, the NHL altered its rules, adopting several innovations designed by the Patrick brothers, Frank and Lester, who had created the Pacific Coast Hockey Association in 1911. Frank established the blue line—an area where there would be no offsides—and legalized forward passing in defensive zones to help maintain the game's flow and excitement. He also pioneered unlimited substitutions, numbered uniforms, penalties for checking into the boards, the penalty shot, freedom of movement for goalies, and a playoff system.

Lester Patrick took on legendary status on April 7, 1928, in the Stanley Cup finals. Then a coach for the New York Rangers, Patrick suddenly found his team without a goalie when, in the second period of Game 2 against the Montreal Maroons, Lorne Chabot suffered an eye injury. Teams did not carry backup goalies, so Patrick asked the Maroons if he could replace Chabot with Ottawa goalie Alex Connell, who was among the thousands of spectators watching the game at the Montreal Forum.

"If you need a goalkeeper, why doesn't Lester play?" was the Maroons' response.

So the silver-haired 44-year-old coach did. He put on Chabot's gear and uniform, added a pair of socks so the skates would fit, and bravely took the ice. The game went into overtime as Patrick deflected a steady round of Maroons' shots. The Rangers' Frank Boucher then stole the puck and scored the game-winner, giving Patrick the victory both as coach and goalie.

The "Silver Fox" was not going to take a chance the rest of the series. The Rangers acquired goalie Joe Miller for the next game and defeated Montreal to win their first Stanley Cup.

The 1929 stock market crash in the United States hurt the NHL. Several teams folded, including the Maroons and the Pittsburgh Pirates. Yet Conn Smythe, general manager of the Toronto Maple Leafs 1929–1961 and one of the game's impresarios, hung on and was able to build Maple Leaf Gardens in five months in 1931. Smythe also first presented hockey "on the air," hiring Foster Hewitt to broadcast games.

Hewitt always greeted listeners, "Hello, Canada, and hockey fans in the United States and Newfoundland." He broadcast his first game on March 22, 1923, via a telephone hookup from a tiny, glass-enclosed booth. The close quarters made it difficult for Hewitt to breathe, but at some point in the game, he yelled what was to become his trademark goal-scoring call: "He shoots! He scores!"

Even though Hewitt vowed the first game would be his last and only broadcast, he stayed behind the microphone for 57 years. At the Maple Leaf Gardens, he worked from a gondola, perched 56 feet above ice level. He broadcast the first televised hockey games in Canada in 1952 and is credited with linking the vast Canadian countryside together with his game reports. The streets of small Canadian towns were empty most Saturday nights because people were inside, listening to Hewitt's voice and "Hockey Night in Canada."

"When I met him years later," said hockey great Bobby Hull, "it was like meeting God."

4 THE FIRST STARS

Hockey's early Canadian heroes captured the imagination of fans on both sides of the border. Today's players skate upon the foundation built by those early stars.

Maurice "The Rocket" Richard was an intense competitor on the ice, but a shy, reserved man away from the game he was born to play. Born in Montreal in 1921, Richard excelled at baseball and boxing as well as his first love, ice hockey. He joined the Canadiens in 1942, at the age of 21.

During the 1944–45 season, Richard did what many thought impossible. He scored 50 goals in just 50 games. Nobody had ever scored more than 44.

"I never knew what I was going to do when I went in until I did it," he said. "If the goaler moved I'd make the play; if he didn't I'd go for one of the corners. If I didn't know what I was going to do, how could the goaltender?"

Richard scored five goals in a game more than once, including a Stanley Cup semifinal game in 1944 against Toronto. "I had only six or seven shots on goal all game," he said that night, "and every goal scored in a different way." He scored all of Montreal's goals in their 5–1 win and was named the game's first, second and third star—postgame honors traditionally given to the three best players in the game.

Eight years later Richard distinguished himself on the ice in an incredible gut-wrenching

Maurice "The Rocket" Richard starred at right wing for the Montreal Canadiens for 18 years. "When he was coming down on you, his eyes were flashing and gleaming like the lights of a pinball machine," said Chicago goalie Glenn Hall. "It was frightening."

performance. On April 8, 1952, the Canadiens and Boston Bruins met in the seventh game of their semifinal playoff. In the second period, Richard collided with Bruins defenseman Bill Quackenbush and cracked his head on the ice. The Rocket was carried unconscious to the dressing room. He returned to the bench in the third period, a bandage covering a six-inch gash over his left eye. He claimed he was fine, but Montreal coach Dick Irvin knew better.

Still, with four minutes left and the game tied 1–1, Irvin sent Richard back onto the ice. Teammate Butch Bouchard fed the Rocket a pass near the Montreal net. Richard, blood streaming down his face, skated toward center ice. He swept around one player, then bullied his way through Quackenbush and fired a low shot for the game-winning goal. The 14,598 Montreal fans erupted into cheers, throwing programs, hats, and whatever they could lift onto the ice.

"Only a guy like the Rocket can score a goal like that," Irvin said.

Richard was devoted to Montreal fans, who rabidly supported him. On March 17, 1955, a riot broke out at the Montreal Forum after he was suspended for the remainder of the season by NHL president Clarence Campbell for his part in a vicious stick fight with Boston's Hal Laycoe.

Richard never won a scoring title, but he was the first to score 500 goals in his career. The Canadiens made the playoffs 15 times in his 18 seasons; their eight Stanley Cup victories included five in a row from 1955 to 1960. The Hockey Hall of Fame has an entire wing devoted to Maurice Richard, who was inducted in 1961.

As Richard's career was ending, another Montreal skater was distinguishing himself in a different way. Goalie Jacques Plante had endured two broken cheekbones, four broken noses and a fractured skull during his career. On November 1, 1959, Plante was having a seven-inch gash under his nose stitched closed when he said, "Enough. I won't go back in without a mask." His coach, Toe Blake, had refused to let him wear a mask because he believed it limited the goalie's vision. But Blake finally gave in, and the mask became a regular part of the goalie's gear.

Plante revolutionized the way the position was played. He was the first to regularly leave the crease and handle the puck. He had become a goalie at 6 because he had asthma, which restricted his breathing and made skating difficult. Plante won seven Vezina Trophies as the league's top goaltender and had 82 career shutouts and 434 wins in 19 years. He was inducted into the Hockey Hall of Fame in 1978.

Jean Beliveau received his first pair of skates at the age of 5. Seventeen years later the Quebec native was playing for a local semipro team in the Quebec Senior League. The Montreal Canadiens wanted him so much they bought the entire league to sign him.

Beliveau did not disappoint them. "Le Gros Bill" led Montreal to 10 Stanley Cups in 18 seasons. In the seven-game final against the Chicago Blackhawks in 1965, he scored the winning goal three times and assisted the other. Over 18 years he averaged 1.08 goals per game in the regular season and playoffs. Beliveau entered the Hall of Fame in 1972.

Gordie Howe gave his life to hockey after fate brought him a pair of skates at his home in Floral, Saskatchewan. A woman seeking money to buy milk for her children sold Howe's mother a sack filled with trinkets, including a pair of ice skates. The 6-year-old Howe shared the new toy with his sister Edna, each using one skate to glide over a frozen potato patch. It was not long before Gordie claimed both skates. He tied magazine catalogs onto his legs for makeshift pads.

Howe was 17, playing in a junior league, when a Detroit scout signed him for a $2,600 salary and a team jacket for a bonus. After one minor league season, he became an instant star in 1949-50. But it almost ended overnight. On March 28, 1950, he crashed face-first into the boards in the opening game of Detroit's semi-final against Toronto. He suffered a broken nose and cheekbone, fractured skull, and scratched eyeball. Doctors feared there might be brain damage that would end his career.

But Howe survived and returned the next season to lead the league in goals, assists, and points. He was ambidextrous and could stick-handle with either hand. If a defenseman tried to check Howe on the right side, he was strong enough to switch his stick to the left hand and shoot from that side.

"Hockey has many superstars," said Detroit coach Jack Adams. "But it has only one super-man. And that's Gordie Howe."

The most dominant right winger in the game, Howe retired in 1971 holding almost every NHL offensive record. Inducted into the

Hall of Fame in 1972, he missed being on the ice and the next year joined his sons, Mark and Marty, in the World Hockey Association. They played together for six years. But even that wasn't enough for Gordie Howe. At the age of 51 he returned to the NHL and played 80 games for the Hartford Whalers, scoring 15 goals in 1979-80. His two sons joined the Whalers on March 12, 1980, making them the first father-son combination to play in the NHL together.

Known everywhere as "Mr. Hockey," Howe played for 32 years over five decades, racking up 1,071 goals and 2,589 points in 2,421 games.

Bobby Hull received his first pair of skates as a Christmas present when he was four years old in Port Anne, Ontario. His sisters taught him how to skate. Hull spent his winters on the ice and his summers on relatives' farms chopping wood, baling hay, and digging ditches.

Suspended by his junior hockey coach for indifferent play and hogging the puck, Hull went home and complained to his father. But his dad agreed with the coach and Bobby returned to the team and apologized. Both Hull and hockey benefited from the experience.

Only Rocket Richard and Bernie "Boom-Boom" Geoffrion had managed to score 50 goals in a season before Hull, the "Golden Jet," burst onto the scene. On March 12, 1966, Hull scored his 51st goal before 21,000 screaming worshippers in Chicago Stadium. Play was halted as the fans gave Hull a seven-minute ovation. Hull finished with 54 goals, and went on to top 50 five times.

In 1972 Hull became the first million-dollar hockey star when he signed with the World

Hockey Association. He entered the Hall of Fame in 1973.

Phil Esposito of the Boston Bruins became the first NHL player to top 100 points, in 1968–69, and the fastest to reach 500 goals. Esposito did not take up skating until he was a teenager in Sault Ste. Marie, Ontario. Not a skilled stickhandler or graceful skater, Esposito scored most of his goals off rebounds of missed shots by his teammates, which earned him the nickname "garbage man."

The Bruins had another potent scoring threat from an unlikely position. Bobby Orr, a solid defenseman, broke out of the position's traditional role to score 1.393 points per game in a career cut short at the age of 30 because of knee injuries. Orr, from Parry Sound, Ontario, captured the hearts of New Englanders. Kids everywhere wore his Number 4. In a Boston newspaper poll asking sports fans to name the city's best athlete, Orr won easily over baseball

As a right wing for the Chicago Blackhawks in the 1960s, Bobby Hull was one of the fastest skaters in the game. His cannon-like slapshot was timed at 118 miles an hour.

stars Ted Williams and Carl Yastrzemski and basketball legends Bob Cousy and Bill Russell.

Orr and Esposito are both in the Hockey Hall of Fame.

Glenn Hall was hockey's iron man, noted for being nearly indestructible despite being so nervous he was sick before every game. Born in Saskatchewan in 1931, Hall started out as a forward. When he was 10, the team goalie was hurt. Nobody else wanted the job, so Hall put on the pads and never left the crease. He played 502 consecutive NHL games from 1955 until 1962, when a back injury sidelined him. With Detroit and Chicago he had not missed a minute of action during that time.

Hall perfected the butterfly style, in which he dropped to his knees and fanned out his pads to cover as much of the net as possible. He played in 115 Stanley Cup playoff games, and entered the Hockey Hall of Fame in 1975.

Guy Lafleur, whose name means "The Flower," skated with the grace and power of a ballet dancer. He bloomed in the 1974–75 season with Montreal, posting the first of six straight years of at least 50 goals and 100 points. When the Canadiens won the Stanley Cup in 1978, Lafleur borrowed the trophy and displayed it on the front lawn of his home so friends and neighbors could see it.

After his induction into the Hall of Fame in 1988, Lafleur returned for one season with the New York Rangers, then went home to Quebec and played three more years for the Nordiques. When he finally retired in 1992, he left this message, "Play every game as if it were your last."

5 POSTWAR GROWTH

World War II had a significant impact on professional hockey. By the 1942–43 season, almost half the NHL—90 players—were in military uniforms. The only teams to survive were the Montreal Canadiens, Toronto Maple Leafs, Boston Bruins, New York Rangers, Detroit Red Wings, and Chicago Blackhawks.

The game also changed at this time. For the 1943–44 season, the NHL wanted more speed in the game and introduced the red line at center ice. Before this rule, forwards had to touch the puck at their own blue line to avoid being called offsides before continuing up the ice. The red line permitted long passes from behind the net to center ice. This boosted the demand for fleet forwards and enabled defensemen to become more creative.

Frank Calder, who had been the NHL president since the league's beginning in 1917, died in Montreal in 1943. Three years later, Clarence Campbell began the first of his 31 years as the league's chief.

The first NHL All-Star game was played in the 1947–48 season to raise money for the league's pension fund. In the inaugural game on Oct. 13, 1947, in Toronto, a team of All-Stars coached by Dick Irvine defeated the reigning Stanley Cup champion Maple Leafs 4–3.

Toronto won three consecutive Stanley Cups in 1947, '48, and '49, the first NHL team to do so.

Goalies were forbidden to wear masks until Jacques Plante of the Canadiens said, "Enough." After taking a puck in the face in the first period of a 1959 game against the Rangers, he put on a plastic mask he had designed and returned to the ice.

Their home ice, Maple Leaf Gardens, took care of the fans, too. The Toronto arena was the first to install protective glass at the top of the rink wall in 1948, and the officials added escalators in 1955 and separate penalty boxes in 1963.

Detroit dominated the league in the 1950s, fueled by the "Production Line" of Gordie Howe, Ted Lindsay, Sid Abel, and goalie Terry Sawchuk. The Red Wings won the Stanley Cup five times from 1942 to '55.

Television expanded the game's exposure. Live televised hockey broadcasts began in Canada with the first "Hockey Night in Canada" from Maple Leaf Gardens on Nov. 1, 1952. The new medium also prompted a wardrobe change for referees. Hockey officials had worn orange sweaters to distinguish themselves from the players. In 1955, referees began wearing shirts with vertical black and white stripes because the orange tops had looked black on the black and white television sets.

The Blackhawks' Stan Mikita, the first Czechoslovakian-born player in the NHL, is credited with inventing the curved hockey stick, although he did so by accident. During a practice, Mikita became angry and tried to break his stick but it wouldn't snap. The blade did curve, and Mikita started shooting pucks at the net with his mangled stick. The variation made the puck slide and dip like a pitcher's fastball.

The game's directors wanted to stay competitive against the National Basketball Association and the National Football League in the battle for fans' sports dollars. In 1967 they added six new teams: the Los Angeles

Kings, St. Louis Blues, Minnesota North Stars, Oakland Seals, Pittsburgh Penguins, and Philadelphia Flyers. The new teams formed the Western Division.

In 1970, the NHL granted franchises to Vancouver and Buffalo, N.Y. The Philadelphia Flyers became the first expansion team to win the Stanley Cup when they beat Boston in six games in 1974. The next season, the Flyers repeated against the Buffalo Sabres. It was the first time in more than 30 years that an Original Six team did not play in the Stanley Cup final.

The success of the expansion teams resulted in the formation of a rival pro hockey league. In 1972, the World Hockey Association (WHA)

The action around the net heats up as Toronto right wing Ron Stewart (12) tries to blast the puck past the prone Jacques Plante. Plante blocked the shot and the Canadiens defeated the Maple Leafs to win the championship in 1959 for the fourth straight year.

was created, making its biggest splash when it signed Hull for an incredible $2.75 million. The WHA imported European players and competed with the NHL for seven years before folding.

Quebec, Edmonton, Winnipeg, and Hartford were absorbed from the collapsed WHA in 1979.

The NHL had added the New York Islanders in 1972 and the Washington Capitals in 1974. The Atlanta Flames transferred to Calgary in 1980. In 1982, the Colorado Rockies relocated to New Jersey, but pro hockey returned to Denver in 1995 when the Quebec franchise transferred to the Rocky Mountain state. The newly christened Colorado Avalanche won the Stanley Cup in 1996, their first year in Denver.

Hockey is the fastest, roughest professional team sport. The frequent body checks and collisions often lead to fights. A time out penalty for a player can leave his team short-handed until he can return to the game.

The addition of San Jose, Tampa Bay, and Ottawa raised the roster to 24 teams.

Expansion opened the way for more European players. Swedish defenseman Borje Salming was the first European player to make an impact on the NHL, playing 17 seasons with Toronto and Detroit, beginning in 1974.

Hockey's growth brought problems. On April 1, 1992, the NHL players went on strike for the first time. They settled 11 days later, receiving meager financial gains. The fans did not seem to care that the game had resumed. Attendance for the remaining 30 games of the season dropped drastically and stayed low throughout the playoffs.

Labor problems returned in 1994–95. The season began with a 103-day lockout in a dispute between players and management. Games finally began in January, but the season was reduced to 48 games and the playoffs extended until June 24.

Wayne Gretzky began skating when he was just 2 years old, scrambling around the ice on tiny skates secured with a leather strap and metal buckle. Once he started competitive hockey against kids in his native Ontario, Gretzky challenged older, more experienced players. He first wore No. 9 in honor of his idol, Gordie Howe, but when Gretzky joined the Sault Ste. Marie Greyhounds junior team, another player had that number. Gretzky wound up wearing No. 99 and it became his trademark.

The gifted skater played just one year of junior hockey in Canada, scoring 70 goals and 182 points in 64 games for the Greyhounds. He then signed a million-dollar contract with Indianapolis of the World Hockey Association. After only eight games, the Edmonton Oilers bought him.

Beginning in 1981, Gretzky won the next seven Art Ross awards, doing so in remarkable record-setting fashion. "The Great One" scored an NHL record 92 goals and 212 points in 1982, becoming the first player to surpass 200 points in a season.

The Oilers were successful, too, winning four Stanley Cups in Gretzky's nine brilliant seasons. But team owner Peter Pocklington had financial troubles, and on August 9, 1988, he traded Gretzky to the Los Angeles Kings for $15 million. In Ottawa, Canada, a member of the Canadian

"Super Mario" Lemieux of the Pittsburgh Penguins won the scoring title in 1993 despite missing part of the season because of Hodgkin's disease. Here he leaves Minnesota goalie Jon Casey in a heap after scoring in a 1991 game.

Parliament asked the government to try to block the trade, saying Gretzky was "as much a national symbol as the beaver."

Gretzky continued his amazing scoring pace and revived interest in the game of hockey in the U.S. and especially in California. He won his ninth Art Ross trophy in 1991 and another in '94 when he led the league with 130 points.

A potentially career-threatening back injury hampered him during the 1992–93 season and the Kings finished 39–35–10, entering the playoffs as the third-place team. But Gretzky led the Kings to the finals against Montreal, which won the Stanley Cup in five games.

Gretzky could not possibly fit all the awards he had accumulated in one room. The Great One established more than 60 scoring records for regular season, playoff, career, and single games, and won nine Hart trophies as the game's most valuable player, two Conn Smythe trophies for playoff MVP, and four Lady Byng trophies for sportsmanship.

How did Gretzky do it? Howe, his friend and admirer, said No. 99 was always moving, always trying to get open for opportunities. Gretzky also had great hands, and often practiced using a tennis ball for a puck to improve his quickness.

"He certainly doesn't have the hardest shot in the game but he picks and hits such precise targets," Howe said. "When you couple that kind of accuracy with his extra quick release, he almost has the goalies beaten before he shoots, especially when he picks the upper corners of the net. Great scorers like Gretzky see open net immediately. The others see the goalie."

In 1996, Gretzky was the highest paid player in the NHL, earning more than $6.5 million. But after a half season with St. Louis, he became a free agent on July 1, 1996, and signed a two-year contract to play for the New York Rangers, reuniting him with former Oilers teammate and close friend Mark Messier.

Ever since he first put on a pair of skates, Brett Hull had to deal with great expectations as the son of hockey legend Bobby Hull, the Golden Jet and Hall of Fame player who may be the best left wing in the game's history.

At the age of 26, Brett Hull became the fifth player in hockey history to reach 50 goals within the first 50 games of a season. It was a feat even his father had not accomplished. The young Hull scored 86 goals that season for the St. Louis Blues, the third highest in NHL history behind Gretzky's seasons of 92 and 87.

Hull actually had a slow start in the game. At 18, he was still playing at the junior hockey level. He played two seasons at the University of Minnesota–Duluth, was drafted 117th by the Calgary Flames of the American Hockey League in 1984, and traded to St. Louis at the end of the 1987-88 season. He scored 41 goals in his first full season with the Blues, but coach Brian Sutter was concerned about Hull's commitment to the game as well as the 20 extra pounds he had gained.

Sutter told Hull to raise his standards, not try to match his father's. It worked.

Hull led the league with 72 goals in 1989-90, and the next season scored 86 to win the Hart Trophy as the NHL's most valuable player. His father had won the award in 1964–65 and 1965–66. They became the first father-son MVP winners, possibly in any pro sport.

"Maybe one day I will be equal to my dad but never better," Brett Hull said. "I will always be Bobby's son."

Mario Lemieux will always be known as "Super Mario" in Pittsburgh. The gifted center led the Penguins to consecutive Stanley Cup championships in 1990–91 and 1991–92 despite intense physical hardship. He had endeared himself to Pittsburgh fans on December 31, 1988, when he recorded his first five-goal game and became the first to shoot for the cycle. Lemieux scored in every conceivable fashion: he scored a goal at even strength, a power-play goal, a short-handed goal, a penalty shot, and an empty-net goal.

At the beginning of the '90–91 season, Lemieux was bedridden following surgery to repair a herniated disk. He missed 50 regular season games but shined in the playoffs, leading all players with 16 goals and 28 assists for 44 points, second only to the 47 compiled by Gretzky in 1985 with the Edmonton Oilers. In the six-game Cup series against Minnesota, Lemieux scored five goals and seven assists to win the Conn Smythe Trophy as Most Valuable Player in the playoffs. His sore back, which often made it too painful for him to even lace up his own skates, forced him to sit out Game 3 of the final, which Pittsburgh lost.

In 1992, Lemieux suffered a broken bone in his wrist in Game 2 of the second round of the playoffs against the New York Rangers, yet came back and totaled 34 points in the play-offs to win his second Conn Smythe Trophy.

Lemieux had to deal with more adversity in the 1992–93 season. He was diagnosed with Hodgkin's disease, a sometimes fatal illness that is marked by enlargement of the lymph nodes, spleen and liver. The Montreal native missed 62 games the next season and decided to retire because he was not 100 percent healthy. But Lemieux had a remarkable recovery and in 1995–96, he was back on the ice for the Penguins. In 1997, "Super Mario" retired for good.

Before Lemieux brought the Cup to Pittsburgh, it was in the hands of the New York Islanders for four consecutive seasons beginning in 1979. The Islanders won just 12 and 19 games in their first two seasons after they came into the NHL in 1972–73. Mike Bossy and Bryan Trottier changed all that. Vancouver coach Roger Neilson called Trottier the best player in the world and said Bossy was the game's greatest scorer.

Neither Trottier nor Bossy had any minor-league experience when they joined the Islanders. Trottier set an NHL record on December 23, 1978, by scoring six points in a single period, including three goals, in the Islanders' 9–4 win over the New York Rangers. On February 13, 1982, he became the seventh NHL player to score four goals in a period during an 8–2 victory over Philadelphia.

Bossy scored 53 goals his first year, and followed with 69 goals the next year to set a record for right wings.

But Bossy was not known only for his goal-scoring abilities. He campaigned for a kinder, gentler game with the focus more on stick-handling and scoring than brawling and

New York Rangers captain Mark Messier holds up the Stanley Cup after the Rangers defeated Vancouver in 1994. Messier was also the captain of the Edmonton Oilers 1990 Stanley Cup champions.

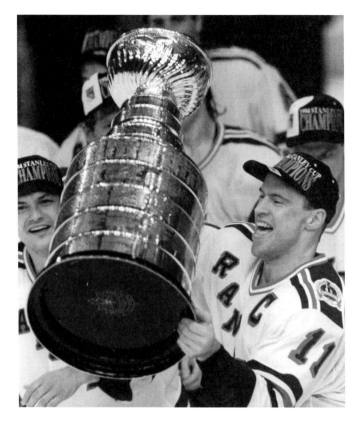

goons. His efforts did not go unnoticed. Bossy won the Lady Byng Trophy for sportsmanship three times.

Chronic back injuries forced him to retire after he missed the entire 1987–88 season, but not until he had helped the Islanders achieve dynasty status with their four consecutive Cup triumphs. In 1980, Bossy scored 10 goals in 16 playoff games, and the next year, he led all playoff scorers and set a record with 35 points in 18 games. In both 1982 and '83, he won the Conn Smythe Trophy as the playoff MVP.

The Penguins recognized Trottier's expertise and he skated for Pittsburgh for two seasons, winning two more Stanley Cups with Lemieux's team. Trottier rejoined the Islanders for one more season, 1993–94, before retiring as the team's all-time leading scorer with 524 goals, 901 assists and 1,425 points.

Mark Messier is the only player to captain two different Stanley Cup championship teams. Messier took the Edmonton Oilers to their fifth playoff title in seven years in 1990, then helped the New York Rangers win it all in 1994, their first championship in 54 years.

A native of Edmonton, Messier was signed by the Indianapolis Racers at the age of 17—after one year of junior hockey—to replace Gretzky, who had just joined the Oilers. In his first season at Indianapolis, Messier scored just one goal in 52 games and that was on a shot from center ice.

He didn't give up and Edmonton saw promise in the wing who joined the Oilers in 1979–80. Gretzky and Messier skated together in Edmonton's glory days in the 1980s. When Gretzky departed for Los Angeles in 1988 many thought the Oilers were finished. But Messier rallied Edmonton to another championship in 1989–90 before leaving for New York in 1991 in a four-player swap. He won his second Hart Trophy for most valuable player in 1992 (he also won in 1990), and his veteran leadership as well as his talented playmaking abilities helped the Rangers win the Cup in '94.

High-powered scorers were not hockey's only stars. Goalie Patrick Roy grew up in Quebec City and seemed destined to play for the Montreal Canadiens. The 51st player selected in the 1984 draft, Roy had a solid rookie season (23–18–3 in 47 games) and was one of eight first-year players on the roster for the Canadiens, who finished seventh that year.

No one expected the Canadiens to win. But Montreal made the playoffs and that's when Roy shined. He won 15 games and compiled a 1.92 goals against average. Only 20 years old, Roy dominated the postseason, showing no signs of being intimidated as Montreal won its 23rd Stanley Cup championship. He was named recipient of the Conn Smythe Trophy, the playoff MVP award.

But those playoff games were relatively easy compared to 1993. That year, Roy won 10 games in sudden death overtime, including three in the finals against Los Angeles. He won 16 games in the postseason to earn his second Conn Smythe Trophy.

Roy won three Vezina Trophies as the league's top goaltender in 1989, '90, and '92 for Montreal before being traded to Colorado.

In 1972, Toronto scout Gerry McNamara, overseas to scout European players, arrived in Stockholm, Sweden, to look at a goaltender. But McNamara saw a defenseman he would call "a once in a lifetime find."

The NHL had expanded to 21 teams and most general managers were discovering that Canada could not supply enough quality players for every team. Sweden was not considered a hockey hotbed because critics felt the players could not survive in the rugged NHL.

On May 12, 1973, Borje Salming and fellow Swede Inge Hammarstrom agreed to join the Maple Leafs. Born in Kiruna, Sweden, Salming struggled at first in the rough and tough NHL and was called a "chicken Swede" for not defending himself. He did his best to shed that label. In Salming's second season with Toronto, 1974–75, he won the inaugural Moulson Cup which was presented to the player who had accumulated the most points via the game's three-star selection. Salming won the Moulson Cup, four of the first seven years it was awarded.

He took his share of hits—and kicks. In 1985–86, Salming was accidently kicked by another player in a goalmouth scramble and suffered a gruesome facial injury. He needed more than 100 stitches to close a gash that ran from his forehead, between his eyes, across the bridge of his nose and into one cheek. Salming returned to the ice wearing a plexiglass face shield on his helmet for protection.

Salming was a unique defenseman because he participated in the offensive attack, upsetting the other team's defensive scheme. He originally was nicknamed "B.J." by his Toronto teammates because they had trouble pronouncing his first name. But eventually, everyone knew him as "King." Salming acquired that moniker one day during practice when he apparently got away with something the others had not.

"Who do you think you are, the King of Sweden?" a smart aleck Maple Leafs teammate quipped.

The nickname stuck.

On Jan. 4, 1988, Salming became the first European player to appear in 1,000 NHL games. A superb defender, Salming also was an excellent puck handler. He ended his career in 1988-89 as the Maple Leafs' career leader in assists and goals by a defenseman. Over 17 seasons with Toronto and Detroit, Salming scored 150 goals. He also tallied 12 goals and 49 points in 81 Stanley Cup playoff games.

7 THE RECORD SETTERS

Wayne Gretzky may have single-handedly rewritten the National Hockey League record book over his career but any discussion on record-setting in the game must begin with Joe Malone.

Malone, born in Quebec City, Quebec, on February 28, 1890, was hockey's first offensive superstar. Known as "The Phantom" because of his lightning-fast moves on skates, Malone joined the Montreal Canadiens in 1917–18 in the NHL's first year. At that time, the league consisted of four teams: Ottawa, Toronto, the Montreal Wanderers, and the Canadiens.

Malone did not waste any time establishing himself. He scored five goals on opening night and finished his debut season with 44 goals in 20 games, an average of more than two goals a game.

His single-season record stood until the 1944–45 season when Maurice Richard scored 50 goals in 50 games. "The Rocket's" record was tied by Montreal's Bernie Geoffrion in the 1960–61 season, and again by Chicago's Bobby Hull in the 1961–62 season.

Hull, known as the "Golden Jet," launched an unprecedented offensive attack in the 1965–66 season when he scored 54 goals for the Black-hawks. He tallied his 51st on March 12, 1966, against the New York Rangers. Hull followed that feat with a 58-goal effort in the 1968–69 season, but Boston's Phil Esposito eclipsed that mark in 1970–71 when he scored 76 goals in 78 games.

Three Hall of Famers for the Montreal Canadiens get together on the ice: (from left) Maurice "Rocket" Richard, Guy Lafleur, and Bernie "Boom Boom" Geoffrion.

However, no one surpassed Richard's 50-goals-in-50-games until the 1981–82 season when a 20-year-old phenom scored 50 goals in 39 games for the Edmonton Oilers. His name was Wayne Gretzky.

Gretzky did not stop at 50 that season. "The Great One" broke Esposito's single-season mark with an incredible 92 goals in an 80-game schedule.

The single-season scoring record is one of the 60-plus records Gretzky owned or shared. He became hockey's all-time leader in points (total goals and assists), goals scored, and assists.

Malone, though, has one record that not even "The Great One" is expected to break. On January 31, 1920, "The Phantom" scored seven goals in a single game against the Toronto St. Pats, including three goals within 120 seconds.

"The goalies used to stand up more in those days," said Malone, who played practically the entire game. "I remember pulling the goalie out a lot. Now they have such scrambles around the goal that most times you have to wait for the red light to go on before you know there's been a goal scored."

Another record that will probably stand forever was set by the Chicago Blackhawks' Bill Mosienko on March 23, 1952. It was the last day of the season and Mosienko scored three goals in 21 seconds—the quickest hat trick ever. Mosienko missed a chance at a fourth goal minutes later when his shot attempt hit the post.

One goalie who distinguished himself in the net was Terry Sawchuk. A native of Winnipeg, Manitoba, Sawchuk started as a center but was asked to play goal because he had a set of pads at home. Those pads belonged to his older brother, who had died of a heart ailment. Sawchuk had a good first game and never left the net.

He signed a pro contract with the Detroit Red Wings when he was just 16 years old. He joined the Red Wings in 1949 and started his second game for Detroit the day Hall of Fame goalie George Hainsworth was killed in a car accident. Eleven years later, Sawchuk would pass Hainsworth's record of 94 NHL shutouts.

In Sawchuk's first season in Detroit, he won 44 games, including 11 shutouts, and posted a 1.99 goals against average to win the Calder Trophy as the league's top rookie.

In his 21-year career, Sawchuk set three NHL records that may never be challenged. He appeared in more games (971) than any other goalie, played the most minutes (57,184) and, most impressive of all, posted the most shutouts (103). The all-time leader in wins with 435, Sawchuk, who played for Boston, Toronto, Los Angeles, and the New York Rangers during his lengthy career, won 44 times in a 70-game schedule in consecutive seasons (1951 and 1952). Only Bernie Parent won more games in a season (47 in 1973–74).

Goalie Glenn Hall secured his spot in the record book by playing in 502 consecutive games from 1955 to 1963, more than any other netminder in NHL history.

However, Gordie Howe is hockey's longevity leader. Howe was the NHL's all-time leading scorer for 29 years, the longest reign in the history of the game. "Mr. Hockey" scored 801 goals, 1,049 assists, and 1,850 points in the NHL, playing primarily for the Detroit Red Wings.

Gordie Howe skated in hockey action in five decades beginning in the 1940s. In 1973 he joined his sons Marty (center) and Mark (right) on the Houston Aeros of the World Hockey Association.

Howe also is the only player to skate in the NHL in five decades, beginning in the 1940s, and he nearly made it six on April 1, 1997, when he was to don his pads again for a minor league team. However, the idea was shelved because the team was in a playoff battle and didn't want any disruptions.

Howe played in more games (1,767) and for more seasons (26) than any other player, and he surpassed all of Maurice Richard's scoring records.

Darryl Sittler did something neither Howe nor Richard nor anyone else ever matched. He became a standout center for the Toronto Maple Leafs and distinguished himself on February 7, 1976, with an offensive barrage, scoring six goals and four assists for an unbelievable 10-point game. Sittler's outburst helped the Leafs defeat the Boston Bruins 11–4 and topped Richard's 1944 record of eight points (five goals and three assists).

Joey Mullen, who grew up in New York City, loved the game and learned to play by skating on a dry surface at the city's roller rinks. On March 14, 1997, Mullen, a star with the Pittsburgh Penguins, made history when he became the first American to score 500 goals in the NHL.

8 THE FUTURE

In 1997, the NHL faced a future without stars of the magnitude of Mario Lemieux and Wayne Gretzky. Hockey in the United States had received a major boost in interest following the "Miracle on Ice" win at the 1980 Winter Olympics. The underdog U.S. team upset the Soviet Union 4–3, then rallied for a three-goal, third-period comeback against Finland for the gold medal.

But the NHL still struggled to receive the media exposure that pro baseball, basketball, and football enjoyed. Hockey needed that visibility to market its next wave of talent, which included left wing Paul Kariya and center Eric Lindros.

Enter Nike. The shoe company, which showcased stars like Michael Jordan and Ken Griffey Jr. internationally, turned its attention to hockey. After purchasing some Canadian hockey equipment companies, Nike planned to sell rollerblades and accompanying gear so that even if kids could not find a frozen pond, they could still work on their stickhandling in parking lots and schoolyards.

In Canada, skaters could freeze a pond in the backyard in the winter. It was more difficult and expensive to find ice time in the U.S., forcing many youth leagues to play very early on weekend mornings. Canada also had a solid trade program in which families exchanged gear as their kids outgrew skates and sticks.

The NHL began the 1991–92 season with only a one-year, $5.5 million deal with the

The Philadelphia Flyers' Eric Lindros reacts after scoring against Buffalo in the 1997 playoffs. "Nobody's played with the size that he has, along with the skill and the speed," Mark Messier said of Lindros. "That sets him apart from anybody who's ever played the game."

limited cable audience of SportsChannel America. They encouraged teams to jazz up their look to attract a young crowd. The Phoenix Coyotes, the San Jose Sharks, and the Anaheim Mighty Ducks all adopted brightly colored logos. The Chicago Blackhawks, one of hockey's "original six," added a black top to their red home and white away jerseys.

With so many teams reaching the post-season, the NHL season had actually become two: the regular season and the playoffs. Being the top team in the regular season did not always guarantee a Stanley Cup championship. In its first season, San Jose demonstrated that the game may not be the most important selling point. The Sharks lost their first 11 games and finished with a league-low 39 points and a 17–58–5 record. Yet the team sold out every game at San Francisco's Cow Palace and the Sharks' teal-and-black souvenirs were the hottest item in sports.

Hockey also found itself struggling with the same problems that have hampered professional baseball, football, and basketball. Since the advent of free agency, allowing players to search for the best contract, it was difficult for fans to develop any kind of loyalty to one team. Many Blackhawks fans were turned off from the team forever when Bobby Hull left in 1972 to sign a $2.75 million deal with the Winnipeg Jets of the World Hockey Association. In August 1996 a new generation of Blackhawks fans were equally disappointed when favorite forward Jeremy Roenick was traded to Phoenix.

Hockey is and always will be Canada's game. But the future may not be in Canada.

In 1995–96, the Quebec Nordiques moved to Denver to become the Colorado Avalanche and won the Stanley Cup in their first year in the United States. The Winnipeg Jets moved south to Phoenix for the 1996–97 season.

Hockey's future may be linked to Japan. The Vancouver Canucks scheduled a series against the Anaheim Mighty Ducks in Tokyo in October 1997.

Ever since Borje Salming's arrival in 1974 from Sweden, more European players were added to team rosters. In 1989, Sergei Priakin became the first Soviet Union player permitted to sign with an NHL club. He spent three seasons with the Calgary Flames. By 1997 more than 100 Russians were skating in the NHL.

For youngsters in northern climates like Canada and Scandanavia, it's easy to find frozen ponds to play on all winter.

NHL teams enlisted players from Czechoslovakia, Sweden, Finland, Poland, Scotland, Switzerland, Latvia, Norway, Germany, Russia—even Nigeria. Rumun Ndur, a defenseman from the West African country, was on the Boston Bruins' roster at the start of the 1996–97 season.

However, because of the breakup of the Soviet Union, the once powerful Red Army teams and sports development programs were discontinued. More players from Finland, Sweden, and Norway would likely find roster spots in the NHL in years to come.

On September 23, 1992, another source of talent emerged. Manon Rheaume, a 20-year-old goaltender, became the first woman to play in one of the four major pro sports leagues when she played the first period for the NHL expansion Tampa Bay Lightning in an exhibition game. Rheaume faced nine shots and allowed two goals in the game against the

Undaunted by a lack of ice, hockey players in St. Louis turn a shopping center parking lot into a rink and use an upended shopping cart for a goal.

St. Louis Blues. She led the Lightning onto the ice and received a standing ovation from the crowd of 8,223 at the Florida State Fairgrounds Expo Hall.

"For me, it's just a chance to play," Rheaume said before the game. "I want to see what I can do. If I don't try, then I don't know what I can do."

Phil Esposito, the former Boston Bruins star who was Tampa Bay's president and general manager, admitted that playing Rheaume was a publicity stunt. However, she quickly proved that she belonged on the ice.

"Manon does have hockey talent," Esposito said. "She's got hockey sense and hockey talent and guts. Those three make for a hockey player."

She became a goalie at age 5, facing shots from her brothers Martin and Pascal. Rheaume played for Team Canada's women's team and was the first woman to play in the Canadian Hockey League, a farm system that prepares juniors for the NHL.

She eventually played in a minor league NHL game in December 1992. Her success played a pivotal role in the growth of women's hockey in Canada. However, she suffered the first major disappointment in her career in March 1997 when she was dropped from the Canadian national women's team that was to compete in the world championships.

But Manon Rheaume has not ruled out playing goalie in the NHL.

CHRONOLOGY

1893	Lord Stanley buys and donates a silver punch bowl—the Stanley Cup—for $48.67 to be used for hockey competition.
1917	National Hockey League is organized November 22 in Montreal. Montreal Wanderers, Montreal Canadiens, Ottawa Senators, Quebec Bulldogs, and Toronto Arenas join the new league, but Quebec does not start until 1919.
1922	Foster Hewitt broadcasts first NHL game on the radio.
1923	First U.S. franchise granted to Boston for following season.
1926–27	NHL expands to 10-team league with Canadian and American divisions.
1942	Frank Calder, president of the NHL since its inception, dies. The Calder Trophy is established to be presented to outstanding rookie each year. Brooklyn Americans withdraw, leaving NHL with a six-team league (Boston, Chicago, Detroit, Montreal, New York, and Toronto) in place for next 25 years.
1947	First annual All-Star Game played for benefit of players' pension fund. All-Stars defeat Stanley Cup champion Toronto 4–3 on October 13 in Toronto.
1967–68	Six new teams added to NHL: California Seals, Los Angeles Kings, Minnesota North Stars, Philadelphia Flyers, Pittsburgh Penguins, and St. Louis Blues. New teams play in West Division while remaining six teams play in East Division.
1969	The amateur draft is expanded to include all amateur players of qualifying age throughout the world.
1972	Bobby Hull signs a $2.75 million contract with the Winnipeg Jets, jumping to the new World Hockey Association.
1991	San Jose Sharks become the 22nd team.
1992–93	Gary Bettman named first NHL commissioner in February 1993. Ottawa Senators and Tampa Bay Lightning added, making NHL 24-team league.
1993–94	NHL adds Mighty Ducks of Anaheim and Florida Panthers, increasing NHL to 26 teams. Minnesota franchise shifts to Dallas and is named Dallas Stars.
1994–95	Labor disruption forces cancellation of 468 games from October 1, 1994, to January 19, 1995. Clubs play 48-game schedule.
1995–96	Quebec franchise transfers to Denver as the Colorado Avalanche. In first season in Colorado, the Avalanche wins the 1996 Stanley Cup.
1996–97	Winnipeg franchise transfers to Phoenix as Phoenix Coyotes.
1999	Retired player Mario Lemieux buys the Pittsburgh Penguins.

RECORDS (THROUGH 1998–99 SEASON)

MOST GOALS IN ONE SEASON
92 – Wayne Gretzky, Edmonton, 1981–82

MOST ASSISTS IN ONE SEASON
163 – Wayne Gretzky, Edmonton, 1985–86

MOST POINTS IN ONE SEASON
215 – Wayne Gretzky, Edmonton, 1985–86

MOST CAREER GOALS
862 – Wayne Gretzky, Edmonton, Los Angeles, St. Louis, NY Rangers

MOST CAREER ASSISTS
1,843 – Wayne Gretzky, Edmonton, Los Angeles, St. Louis, NY Rangers

MOST CAREER POINTS
2,705 – Wayne Gretzky, Edmonton, Los Angeles, St. Louis, NY Rangers

MOST SEASONS PLAYED
26 – Gordie Howe, Detroit 1946–47 to 1970–71; Hartford 1979–80

MOST GAMES
1,767 – Gordie Howe, Detroit 1946–47 to 1970–71; Hartford 1979–80

MOST GOALS ONE GAME
7 – Joe Malone, Quebec Bulldogs, Jan. 31, 1920, at Quebec

MOST CAREER GAMES APPEARED IN BY GOALTENDER
971 – Terry Sawchuk, Detroit, Boston, Toronto, Los Angeles, NY Rangers,
1949–50 to 1969–70

MOST GAMES ONE SEASON BY A GOALTENDER
79 – Grant Fuhr, Edmonton, 1995–96

MOST CAREER SHUTOUTS BY A GOALTENDER
103 – Terry Sawchuk, Detroit, Boston, Toronto, Los Angeles, NY Rangers,
1949 to 1969–70

MOST SHUTOUTS ONE SEASON BY GOALTENDER
22 – George Hainsworth, Montreal, 1928–29 (44 games played)

MOST WINS ONE SEASON BY GOALTENDER
47 – Bernie Parent, Philadelphia, 1973–74

MOST CAREER WINS BY GOALTENDER
447 – Terry Sawchuk, Detroit, Boston, Toronto, Los Angeles, NY Rangers,
1949 to 1969–70

FURTHER READING

Hollander, Zander. *Complete Encyclopedia of Hockey.* Detroit: Invisible Ink Press, 1992.

Italia, Bob. *100 Unforgettable Moments in Pro Hockey.* Minneapolis: Abou & Daughters, 1996.

Jacobs, Jeff. *Hockey Legends.* New York: M. Friedman Publishing Group, 1995.

Orr, Rank. *Story of Hockey.* New York: Random House, 1971.

Romain, Joseph. *Pictorial History of Hockey.* New York: Smithmark, 1995.

Taylor, Jim. *Gretzky: The Authorized Pictorial History.* Buffalo, NY: Firefly Books, 1994.

INDEX

CARRIE MUSKAT has covered major league baseball since 1981, beginning with United Press International in Minneapolis. She was UPI's lead writer at the 1991 World Series. A freelance journalist since 1992, she is a regular contributer to *USA Today* and *USA Today Baseball Weekly.* Her work also has appeared in the *Chicago Tribune, Inside Sports,* and *ESPN Total Sports Magazine.*

Christian Jr./Sr High School
2100 Greenfield Dr
El Caion. CA 92019